How to Add a Device to My Kindle Account

A Complete Guide on How to Add Kindle Device to My Account, How to Connect Your Digital Devices to Your Amazon Account

MARK HOWARD

Table of Contents

INTRODUCTION   11

CHAPTER 1: HOW TO MAKE YOUR HOUSE AMAZON SMART   15

Amazon Brings Families Together   19

CHAPTER 2: YOUR MUSIC, YOUR WAY, THROUGH AMAZON   29

Connecting to your Amazon account with Android   33

Connecting to Your Amazon Account with IOS   38

CHAPTER 3: LITERATURE THROUGH AMAZON   45

Audiobooks   54

Downloading the Audible App for Your Devices   56

Audible for IOS: 57

Audible for Android: 59

Audible for Windows: 60

CHAPTER 4: AMAZON AS A TV RECEIVER
65

Using your Smart TV	66
Using Your Amazon Fire TV	68
Using Your Amazon Fire Tablet	69
Using Your Gaming Console	70
Using Your IOS Phone/Tablet	72
Using Your Android Phone/Tablet	73
Passport on Your TV	77
What's Next for TV?	79

CHAPTER 5: FREE TIME FOR KIDS AND PARENTS 85

What about the Teens?	96

CHAPTER 6: ALEXA, YOUR PERSONAL ASSISTANT 103

Alexa Plays the Beats	109
What's wrong, Alexa?	112
Alexa Is the New Desktop Assistant	112
Give Alexa an Apple	113
What's on TV, Alexa?	114

Follow the steps below to set up extra Fire TV devices:
115

CONCLUSION 121

CHECK OUT OTHER BOOKS 125

Text Copyright © Mark Howard

All rights reserved. No part of this guide may be reproduced in any form without permission in writing from the publisher except in the case of brief quotations embodied in critical articles or reviews.

Legal & Disclaimer

The information contained in this book and its contents is not designed to replace or take the place of any form of medical or professional advice; and is not meant to replace the need for independent medical, financial, legal or other professional advice or services, as may be required. The content and information in this book has been provided for educational and entertainment purposes only.

The content and information contained in this book has been compiled from sources deemed reliable, and it is accurate to the best of the Author's knowledge, information and belief. However, the Author cannot guarantee its accuracy and validity and cannot be held liable for any errors and/or omissions. Further, changes are periodically made to this book as and when needed. Where appropriate and/or necessary, you must consult a professional (including but not limited to your doctor, attorney, financial advisor or such other professional advisor) before using any of the suggested remedies, techniques, or information in this book.

Upon using the contents and information contained in this book, you agree to hold harmless the Author from and against any damages, costs, and expenses, including any legal fees potentially resulting from the application of any of the information provided by this book. This disclaimer applies to any loss, damages or injury caused by the use and application, whether directly or indirectly, of any advice or information presented, whether for breach of contract, tort, negligence, personal injury, criminal intent, or under any other cause of action.

You agree to accept all risks of using the information presented inside this book.

You agree that by continuing to read this book, where appropriate and/or necessary, you shall consult a professional (including but not limited to your doctor, attorney, or financial advisor or such other advisor as needed) before using any of the suggested remedies, techniques, or information in this book.

Introduction

Congratulations on downloading *How to Add a Device to My Kindle Account* and thank you for doing so. In today's cloud-based world, it is easier than ever to have your entire entertainment library at the touch of a button and what better way than through your Amazon Prime account? By downloading this book, you have given yourself a major advantage in being able to plug into the many benefits available through Amazon.

Your digital accessories are more than equipment; they help you maintain a specific way of living for you and your family. By harnessing the connection power of your phone, TV, tablets, gaming consoles, and just about any other smart device you might have, you'll be well on your way to enjoying the best entertainment in a more convenient way!

The following chapters will discuss the comfort of having all your devices connected; the different devices that are available to connect to your Amazon account, and easy to read instructions on how to connect each device. As technology continues to advance, you can rest easy knowing that you will be ahead of the game in knowledge and understanding of exactly how it all works. Amazon is an amazing colleague in just about every corner of the globe and we want to make sure you are connected in every way possible.

There are plenty of books on this subject on the market, thanks again for choosing this one! Every effort was made to ensure it is full of as much useful information as possible, please enjoy!

Chapter 1: How to Make Your House Amazon Smart

Amazon Prime has been a lifesaver for a lot of modern families. You can buy books, shop for groceries, and have seamless unlimited connections to your favorite online media. In addition to the ever popular fast and free shipping, you can also stream music, your favorite TV shows, read the latest best sellers, and have Alexa order pizza all at the same time. With benefits like this, it's no wonder more and more people are connecting to their Amazon accounts in every way possible.

Nowadays anything can be controlled remotely. From the car to the refrigerator, your entire house can be operated from the touch of a button through apps and voice activating systems. The convenience of being able to monitor everything from the thermostat to the ceiling fans adds an extra level of luxury. There's also the ability to have in-demand information whenever you need it. Things like the date and time are common but what about how much power each device is using? Or maybe for extra security measures you want to check on the security cameras on your property and from your car when you're stuck in traffic?

Technology has come a long way since setting the timer for the coffee pot in the morning. Now you can have the lights, the ice maker, the radio, and the TV all come on at a designated time and you don't even have to get off the couch. Doesn't that sound nice? That's the freedom of having smart technology and being able to customize your house so that it begins to understand exactly how you want things to be.

Amazon is constantly working on ways that they can bring value to its customers and the products they use. Voice command operations and technical programming are just the tip of the iceberg when it comes to connecting your everyday life to Amazon.

Below are some of the best products that help turn your house into a thriving habitat of the future:

- Keep up to date and see real time what is going on in your house with live- feed

cameras, motion notification, and store up to 24-hours of clips.
- No more digging for keys. Use voice commands to lock and unlock your doors.
- Doorbells that use video and face recognition make it easier than ever to see who is visiting.
- Customizable light features let you set the mood with dimming.
- Heating and air conditioning can be adjusted from anywhere in the house.
- Using Bluetooth technology, you can check fuel levels, light codes, and driving distance in your car.

Obviously, there have been a lot of advances in technology and a lot of common activities can be completed through multiple devices, but how do we go about connecting the devices to your Amazon account? We will review the steps required for connecting home devices to your account in a later chapter. In the meantime, let's explore the ways that Amazon has improved the ability to use technology to bring your family together.

Amazon sells everything from common household items like paper towels and toothpaste to French fry holders and horse head masks, but can this book-seller-turned-technology-powerhouse use its leverage to help make family bonds stronger? The economy leader has streamlined everything from music, to fashion, to TV production, but are consumers and profit at the forefront of the plan or is there something bigger at play?

Amazon Brings Families Together

Technology lets us do a lot of things that we never thought imaginable. Within seconds, a simple internet search and we can have times, dates, and other miscellaneous facts about any topic we choose at our fingertips. As technology advances at warp speed, so do the concerns and worries that our electronic devices are tearing families apart.

While Amazon strives to make life more convenient and hassle free with their smart house features, they are also committed to bringing your family together through the means of technology. For example, while you can program your lights and doorbell, you can also call family through the Echo. Voice activated calling could mean staying in touch more with family. Kid friendly Echo calling could mean staying in touch with elderly family or getting the whole family together during holidays even when everyone can't be together at the same place.

Living in a smart house might not be at the forefront of your mind at the moment but don't be too surprised when in the future, you buy a home and Alexa is already occupying her digital space. The voice activated system is a growing popular set up for convenience and as new products make their way to the smart house group, who wouldn't want a smart house?

So, what are some ways you can incorporate smart devices into your everyday schedule? You can buy smart bulbs that are capable of being customized so that they activate from your internet and be controlled remotely.

From there, you can purchase a Smart Lock so that you never have to guess who is visiting your home. You are able to monitor your front door from an app on your phone. You'll be able to lock and unlock your door even if you aren't home and allow certain visitors in and deny others, all with the tap of your finger.

Why stop there? Why not make yourself comfortable in your house and in your wallet? Smart thermostats will not only help keep the temperature regulated in your house, but you can program it so that it comes on when you anticipate being home and goes off when you don't think you'll need it on which will in turn reduce your heating and air conditioning bill. With a smart thermostat, you'll be able to have complete climate control in your house and with your budget.

While none of these features can make your home trouble free, you will have more control and a sense of security that will help set your mind at ease. While comfort and efficiency are obviously very important, your family's safety is even more so, and these products are leaps and bounds ahead. Even if you are on the fence about turning your house into a digital voice-controlled haven, you can't deny the benefits of the convenience and the efficiency of having full control with the swipe of a hand or a simple voice command.

Just like Amazon listens to the demands of the consumers, smart houses – and Alexa – are designed to listen on demand. You want value and Amazon is committed to providing that value. Through comfort, convenience, and energy efficient appliances, by choosing Amazon devices you can rest easy knowing that your family and your house are in good hands.

If you still can't decide on upgrading your traditional devices to their modern digital counterparts, take a look below at some additional smart devices that might just tip you towards the digital age.

Smart Light Switch –
- Turn your lights on and off from anywhere with the touch of a button on your phone. It even adapts to your schedule to automatically turn the lights on and off. Alexa can even operate it for you.

Smart Fork –

- Having trouble sticking to your diet? Wanting to know just how much you're eating down to the bite? This unique kitchen gadget will analyze your eating habits and even give you advice on healthier eating.

Smart Doorbell –

- Expecting the mailman? Waiting for a FedEx or UPS package? Let this digital door greeter let you know who is coming so you can actually remotely answer the door. Never miss a package again.

Smart Toothbrush –

- Want to get the most out of a not-so-exciting task? This little gadget connects to your smartphone using facial detection technology and shows you the teeth you've brushed and ones you didn't.

Smart Pet Feeder –
- Never miss a feeding for your furry friend again. This digital feeder lets you know your pet's eating habits, you can schedule feedings, and it even dispenses food at a slow rate so that your pet has less of a chance of getting sick or bloated. How's that for convenient?

Smart Coffeemaker-

- Programmable coffee makers have become part of the morning routine in most households but this one takes the basic and pushes it to the max. This digital coffee house can be programmed by an app on your phone so that you never have to wait for the brewing to finish again. You can even set it to your alarm so that it's ready to go before you are.

Smart Toilet –

- Even for your throne there is a smart device. This smart toilet comes with a temperature-controlled bidet for cleaning and air-drying. Enough said.

Smart Bed –

- If technology couldn't get any sweeter, the smart bed will have you feeling like you're sleeping on clouds. Not only can you adjust the bed to how firm or soft you like it, but it also tracks your sleeping patterns so that you can get as good a night sleep as possible.

With all these advanced choices for the house, you will be more automated, more secure, and more digital than ever. Not only will you be able to track and monitor everything, but you will know exactly what's going on behind the scenes more now than ever.

Chapter 2: Your Music, Your Way, Through Amazon

Whether you are sitting in traffic, on the subway commuting to the office, or just cleaning up around the house, being able to enjoy your favorite songs should be hassle free. With the benefit of Amazon Prime's Music Catalog, you can enjoy commercial free streaming for hours available through the app. You can set up your custom playlist through Amazon Prime Music on a variety of devices including:

- PC & Mac Computers
- Android & IOS Devices
- Amazon Fire TV

- Roku Devices
- ECHO Devices

There are multiple listening options to choose from like the basic Prime Music plan, the Music Unlimited Echo Plan, the Individual Plan, and the Unlimited Family Plan but once you decide on which is best for you, dive right in listening to your favorite music whenever you want.

To make things even easier, you don't even have to visit a website to sign up for the Music Unlimited Plan. Your Alexa set up will walk you through the entire process. All you have to do is tell her that you want to get the account going and she will guide you along. In a later chapter, we dive farther into all the many benefits that Alexa can bring to your smart house, but for now, here are the basics for how on you can set up your musical experience yourself.

However, if you'd rather have full hands on control of setting up your account, the steps below will walk you through so you'll be well on your way to listening to your favorite tunes.

To set up your music membership:

- Log into your Amazon account – www.amazon.com
- Select the drop-down menu under *Accounts & Lists*
- Select *Memberships and Subscriptions*
- Choose *Music Subscriptions*
- If you've never registered your music subscription you will receive a 30-day free trial. In this section, select *Sign Up*

- Then decide on whether you want the individual plan or the family plan. Your account will automatically connect to your Amazon information and your preferred method.
- Should you decide to cancel, you can do so through the *Music Subscriptions* page.

Your Lists	Your Account
Wish List	Your Account
Shopping List	Your Orders
Books	Your Dash Buttons
	Your Lists
Create a List	Your Recommendations
Find a List or Registry	Your Subscribe & Save Items
Find a Gift	Memberships & Subscriptions
Save Items from the Web	Your Service Requests
Wedding Registry	Your Prime Membership
Baby Registry	Your Garage
Friends & Family Gifting	Your Pets
Pantry Lists	Start a Selling Account
Your Hearts	Register for a Business Account
Explore Idea Lists	Your Amazon Credit Cards
Explore Showroom	Your Content and Devices
Scout	Style Explorer	Your Music Library
	Your Amazon Photos

Now that you have your account set up, let's get your devices connected. With Amazon music, you can have up to 10 devices authorized to your music library at the same time. If you choose to deauthorize a device, you can edit these settings in the Your *Amazon Music Settings* screen. To make it easier, you can also have Amazon automatically deauthorize devices that aren't used within a 90-day period.

Connecting to your Amazon account with Android

When connecting to your Amazon Unlimited Plan for the first time, you will want to download the app through the app store on your Android phone (you will need Android OS version 4.4 or higher). You can also download the app through your device's browser and connect to your Amazon account that way. Just be sure when you're signing in that you use the correct account information so that your acccount is connected properly.

You can also install the Amazon widget once you've connected your account. The widget will make it even easier to listen to your music library. To install the widget on your Android phone, press and hold on a blank section on your Android's home screen until you see a menu pop up at the bottom. Select the Widgets tab and search for Amazon Music and the widget will then be installed.

The Amazon Music app lets you listen to music that you've purchased from the Amazon Music Digital Store as well as music you've previously purchased and downloaded. Below is a breakdown of the features in the app and how to get around so that you can start enjoying your music even faster.

My Music –

- Find purchased and saved music. Previously purchased music or music that you have uploaded can be found under the Online Music tab. Music that has been stored on your phone's SD card can be found under the Offline Music tab. (Select settings and tap Refresh My Music if you aren't seeing some of your music).

Browse –

- Search for music that you've purchased, recent titles you've played or downloaded, or for new titles that you'd like to purchase from the Digital Music Store. You can type in one word or the entire title depending on what you have. Amazon will do the rest.

Playing –

- Once you have the app set to your liking, you can begin enjoying your music. When starting a song, you'll see a 'Now Playing' screen with progress and playback options available. If you decide to continue searching through the app or do something different altogether, you can minimize the 'Now Playing' screen by selecting the 'X' in the top right corner. A small bar with controls will pop up at the bottom of your screen so that you can continue with your music with ease.

If you want to take things a step further, you can download music to listen to in offline playback from the **My Music** tab, shop for music in the **Digital Music Store**, and through the **Amazon Unlimited Plan** and **Prime Music**, you'll be able to reap even more benefits from your Amazon account for your music listening pleasure.

Connecting to Your Amazon Account with IOS

When connecting to your Amazon Unlimited Plan for the first time, you will want to download the app through the app store on your IOS device (you will need IOS version 10.0 or higher). You can also download the app through your devices browser and connect to your Amazon account that way. Just be sure when you're signing in that you use the correct account information so that your acccount is connected properly.

You can also install the Amazon widget once you've connected your account. The widget will make it even easier to listen to your music library. To install the widget on your IOS device, press and hold on a blank section on your phone's home screen until you see a menu pop up at the bottom. Select the

Widgets tab and search for the Amazon Music and the Widget will then be installed.

The Amazon Music app lets you listen to music that you've purchased from the Amazon Music Digital Store as well as music you've previously purchased and downloaded. Below is a breakdown of the features in the app and how to get around so that you can start enjoying your music even faster.

My Music –

- Find purchased and saved music. Previously purchased music or music that you have uploaded can be found under the Online Music Tab. Music that has been stored on your phone's SD card can be found under the Offline Music tab. (Select settings and tap

Refresh My Music if you aren't seeing some of your music).

Browse –

- Search for music that you've purchased, recent titles you've played or downloaded, or for new titles that you'd like to purchase from the Digital Music Store.

Playing –

- Once you have the app set to your liking, you can begin enjoying your music. When starting a song, you'll see a 'Now Playing' screen with progress and playback options available. If you decide to continue searching through the app or do something different altogether, you can minimize the 'Now Playing' screen by selecting the 'X' in the top right corner. A small bar with controls will pop up at the bottom of your screen so that you can continue with your music with ease.

If you want to take things a step further, you can download music to listen to in offline playback mode from the My Music tab, shop for music in the Digital Music Store, and through the Amazon Unlimited Plan and Prime Music, you'll be able to reap even more benefits from your Amazon account for your music listening pleasure.

No matter what device you use, Amazon has you covered when you want to listen to your music at home or on the go. Just download the app and after a few simple clicks, you'll be able to have your music streaming the way you want it. But what if you don't want to pay for a subscription to stream music? Amazon has you covered there too!

To buy digital music there are a few things you need to get taken care of first. Things like an Amazon account, a U.S. billing address, and a payment method like a debit or credit card that you can use for the 1-click purchase that will automatically send your music to your account.

To purchase digital music, follow these steps:
1. Search for the music title or album that you want to buy.
2. Click on the title and open the detail page.
3. Purchase the music
    a. Click buy album or title
    b. Click cart icon
    c. Place order

Go Unlimited
Start your 30-day free trial

Listen to any song, anywhere with Amazon Music Unlimited. Learn More

Buy MP3 Album $9.49

Add to MP3 Cart

You can also use gift cards to make digital music purchases. You just need to input the gift card information into the purchase screen.

Regardless what method you choose, whether you decide to go with a monthly subscription or purchase your songs directly, Amazon Music makes it possible to listen to your favorite songs or albums in a variety of methods.

Chapter 3: Literature through Amazon

Being able to feed your mind is an important part of maintaining a healthy lifestyle. However, with family obligations and everyone always being on the go, who has time to sit down and read a book? Amazon has you covered.

In the early days of Kindle, avid readers were able enjoy the freedom of reading without the storage issues of maintaining a glorious library. Today, that freedom is even more prominent with technology advancements made through computers, tablets, and smartphones. Newspapers, magazines, fiction and non-fiction alike are all available through Amazon Prime Kindle.

Prime Reading is a gateway into a digital world of stories and adventure. By connecting to your Amazon Prime account, you will have access to over 1,000 different titles. In addition to books, you'll also have access to magazines, comics, newspapers, and many more just by connecting your device to your Amazon account through the Kindle app.

While being able to read on the go has its own amazing benefits, Amazon has dedicated a lot of time and effort into perfecting the Kindle app so that its users are able to get the most benefit in a short amount of time. From being able to read on-demand when you download reading material or wanting to save it for later, Amazon has made the Kindle app experience essentially problem free and user friendly.

Gaining access to the Kindle app is simply a process of:

- going into your device's app store
- searching for the app
- downloading the app

What happens after you download the app is going to vary depending on the type of device you are using. Once you download the app, you want to sign in using your specific Amazon account so that all your Kindle information is shared across the Amazon servers. Let's break down the operational process of the app through both Android and IOS devices.

By logging into your Amazon account through the app on your device, you will have access to all your books that you have previously downloaded as well as the ability to add to your collection. Within the app you will have a variety of options that you'll be able to tailor your Kindle experience and have your favorite reading material at your fingertips.

So, you have the app downloaded, your account is connected, and you are ready to start reading. How do you go about finding your favorite reading books, magazines, and newspapers? The best method of starting your digital collection of reading material is to buy them.

Amazon boasts a wide assortment of best sellers, discounted novels, and other informational pieces. Buying books for the Kindle is simply a matter of knowing what you want and how to find it. By following the steps below, you are well on your way to having a digital library any avid reader would be proud of.

Depending on the method by which you'll be reading will determine just exactly how you are going to purchase books through Amazon Kindle. If you are using and IOS device or purchasing from a desktop computer, follow the steps below.

| Purchase Books Through iPhone/iPad/Desktop (Safari, Chrome, IE, etc.) | 1. Open your preferred browser on your device.
 2. Go to https://www.amazon.com/Kindle-eBooks
 3. If need be, log into your desired Amazon account.
 4. Go back to the Kindle eBook screen via the link given above.
 5. Search for the eBook you want to purchase.
 6. Choose the device you |

	want the eBook to be delivered to. 7. Choose ***Buy Now With 1-Click***

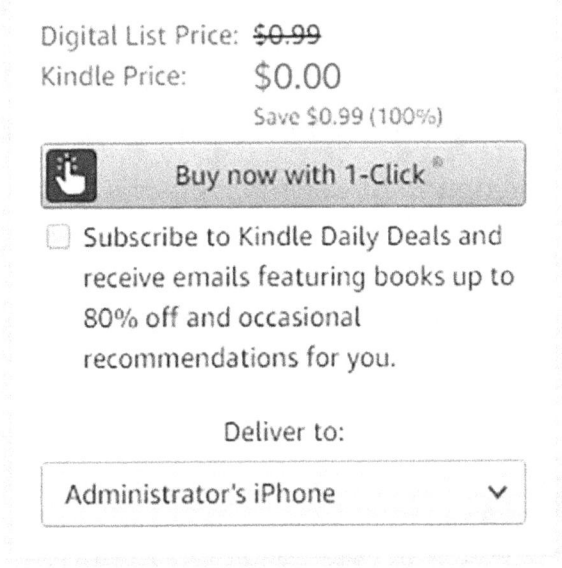

Some books are able to be purchased at no cost. These books are still purchased through the Kindle eBook page and will show as a purchase on your purchase history but there is no fee. You can search for these discounted books by typing in the search box 'Free Kindle Books'.

Once you have purchased at least one book, that book and all the other books that you purchase will be available to download through the Kindle app. Here you will have the option of downloading the book to your device or simply leaving it in the app. You can download as many books to your device as you like but be sure you have enough space.

If you want to find a specific title that you have downloaded, you can use the search feature. This is especially helpful if you have acquired a fairly large collection and don't want to search through each title individually.

Should you find yourself with an overwhelmingly large collection and decide that you want to remove some of the titles that you've purchased; with just a few steps you'll be able to make room for new and exciting titles.

How to remove downloaded books from the Kindle app:

- Open the Kindle app on your device.
- In the upper right corner, select Download
- Touch and hold the title you are wanting to remove
- A prompt box will appear, select 'Remove from Device'

You are now free to add more titles that you have purchased.

Audiobooks

If you're the kind of person that likes to read but find that you just don't have enough time to sit down and enjoy a good book, then maybe audiobooks are the perfect fit for you. A lot of your favorite titles have been turned into audiobooks which give you the convenience of listening without inconveniencing other tasks that you might need to get done. You simply purchase the audiobook, download it, and listen while you go about your day. What could be easier than that?

In addition to the convenience of listening to audiobooks versus reading actual books, there is also the benefit of being able to retain what you hear better than your brain trying to fill the gaps of what you see. Plus, since you're not able to go back and read what you just heard, you are more likely to try harder to retain the information. If you are ready to take the plunge into audiobooks, keep reading to see how easy Amazon has made it through Audible for you to read your favorite books with your ears!

Some Amazon devices are already equipped with Audible like Fire TV and the Echo – Alexa family. Other devices like IOS and Android phones and tablets simply require an app download. The app comes jam-packed with features that are tailored around your busy scheduled. Things like being able to adjust the speed of narration, taking your device with you in the car, and even setting a timer so that the book goes off when you're asleep, so you never miss important parts are all must haves for audiobook aficionados.

Downloading the Audible App for Your Devices

In order to download your favorite book in audio format, you of course have to download the Audible app. You will of course go to your app store on your device and search for the Audible app there. After you download it on your device, follow the steps below to enjoy your audiobooks.

Audible for IOS:

- Sign into the Audible app.
- Select **My Library** on the bottom, and then **Cloud** on the top (its highlighted orange when you are on the right page).

- From the Cloud tab, you will be able to see all the audiobooks you have purchased. If you want to download the book, click on the arrow you see in the bottom-right corner.

- As always before you download anything, make sure you have enough space on your device.
- Once you have downloaded your audiobook, it will no longer be greyed, and you are ready to start listening!

- You can now listen to your audiobook!

Audible for Android:

- Sign into the Audible app.
- Select **My Library** in top left corner.
- Select **Cloud**.

- Select the Audiobook you want to download.
- Select the download icon and download your audiobook.
- As always before you download anything, make sure you have enough space on your device.

- You can now listen to your audiobook!

Audible for Windows:

- Download the app from the Microsoft Store
- Sign in with your account information
- Go to the **My Library** screen
- Select the three dots to the right of the title

- You will see a drop-down box with options that you can choose from. Select download.

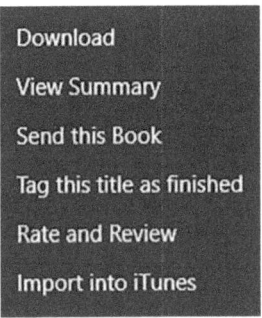

- If you decide you don't want to download the audiobook, but you still want to listen, you now have the option of streaming it through your computer.

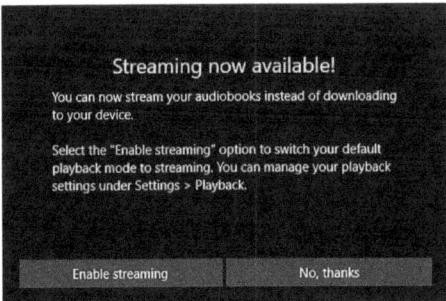

- If you don't see a specific audiobook in your library, you can adjust the filters in the top right corner of the app.

Regardless of which device you use, you always have the option of purchasing directly through the Amazon website https://www.amazon.com/audible. Your purchase will show up in your list the next time you sign into the app on your device.

With the millions of titles available through Audible and Kindle, finding something to read should be no problem. You'll be able to find your old favorites and maybe even some new titles that'll take you on new digital book adventures. The only difficult choice you'll have to make is what title you want to read (or hear) first.

Chapter 4: Amazon as a TV Receiver

With family demands always at the forefront of our minds, there are times when we have the luxury of being able to slow down and just relax. When these unicorns of times do happen, we want to be able to kick back and enjoy our favorite shows or movies. What better way to do that than through the Amazon Prime Video app? Don't have a Smart TV? No problem. Amazon has got you covered there too.

Through either their Amazon Fire TV or the Fire TV Stick, there are many different options to being able to watch your must-have programming through Amazon.

Depending on which device you intend to access Amazon Prime TV through, will determine exactly how you go about connecting to your Amazon account. If you want to access your account through your TV in the living room, follow the easy process below to get your programming streaming in a short amount of time.

Using your Smart TV

Connecting your Smart TV	1. Download the app through the Prime Video App in the app

	store.
2. Open the App.
3. Register your device with Amazon.
4. -You can do this through your TV or through the Amazon website, just enter the code they give you from the website into the

	app on your TV 5. Enjoy!

Using Your Amazon Fire TV

Connecting your Fire TV	1. Turn on the device. 2. Sign in with your already registered Amazon account. 3. Press home button on your device.

	4. Enjoy!

Using Your Amazon Fire Tablet

Connecting your Fire Tablet	1. Turn on the device. 2. Sign in with your already registered Amazon account. 3. Press home button on your device.

	4. Enjoy!

Using Your Gaming Console

Connecting your Gaming Console	1. Download the app through the app store. 2. Open the App. 3. Register your device with Amazon. 4. You can do this

	through your gaming device or through the Amazon website, just enter the code they give you from the website into the app on your console. 5. Enjoy!

Using Your IOS Phone/Tablet

Connecting your IOS Device	1. Download the app through the Prime Video App in the app store. 2. Open the App. 3. Register your device with Amazon. 4. You can do this through your actual device or

	through the Amazon website, just enter the code they give you from the website into the app on your phone or tablet. 5. Enjoy!

Using Your Android Phone/Tablet

Connecting your Android Device	1. Download the app through the Prime Video App in the app store. 2. Open the App. 3. Register your device with Amazon. 4. You can do this through your actual device or through the Amazon

	website, just enter the code they give you from the website into the app on your phone or tablet. 5. Enjoy!

Great, you've now connected your favorite device to your Amazon account but now you've got this fantastic set-up with no idea how to operate it. We've went through all the technical jargon and broken it down into simple steps to get you watching your favorite shows.

With Amazon TV, you are able to rent or purchase digital versions of thousands of shows and movies all from the comfort of your living room. With your Amazon Prime membership, you can reap the benefit of Amazon's original programming as well as other exclusive content available only to Prime members.

When you stream directly through your TV, you are able to view in standard, high definition, or 4K depending on your setup. You are able to download rentals and purchases for offline viewing as well as some of the Prime only content as well. Granted you are limited to just two films or shows at the same time and you have 48 hours to watch the program once you start, but that's an awesome benefit that other providers don't offer. This is especially beneficial when you are travelling in places that have limited or no internet service available.

Passport on Your TV

The safety of your children is very important that's why Amazon has made it easier than ever to add your PBS Passport account to your Amazon Fire TV or Android Smart TV for streaming access.

To get started, go to:

- http://www.pbs.org/activate into your browser
- Activate your PBS Passport account
- Open the PBS channel on your Amazon or Android device

- On the left side, open the settings menu
- At the bottom of the screen, choose Change Account
- You will be prompted to choose which account to log in/out with
- Choose the account you wish to log out of
- A prompt box will open giving you the option to Activate – click Activate
- You will be given a 7-character activation code
- Go back to your computer and type http://pbs.org/activate into your browser
- Enter the activation code you were given prior (NOTE: this is NOT your Passport Activation code)
- Select Continue

- You will then be taken to a new page where you can log in with your Google, Facebook, or PBS account
- Use the same account you used to create your Passport account
- It is important you use the same account you created or will not be able to view Passport programming
- Once you sign in, your device is activated

What's Next for TV?

While there are so many innovative things you can do now with Amazon TV, what does the digital retail giant have in store to stay on the top of the entertainment connection? From picture quality to enhance sound and improved voice activation, Amazon has announced a lot of new plans in the works to take their TV devices even further.

Before we explore what's coming next, what are the must haves for Amazon TV now? If you want your Smart TV to get even smarter, why not try to the Amazon Fire TV Cube? With the Cube, you can control your TV, speakers, and cable connecter all with a few voice commands. Want to change the channel, raise or lower the volume, do some Amazon shopping? The Cube will let you do all that and more without ever using your hands. Talk about shopping adventure of the future!

The Cube eliminates all the excess controls simply by communicating with Alexa and being able to turn to your chosen channel. And hookup is as easy as pulling it out of a box and plugging it up. All you'll need is an HDMI cable and then Amazon's easy on screen set up guide will take you through each step the entire way. What could be easier than that? The next thing you know, this little box is controlling your entire entertainment center and you have never have to go searching for a remote control again.

The Amazon Fire TV Cube even recognizes other apps like Netflix and Hulu, too. The Cube can even control them. All you have to do is tell Alexa to "Open Netflix" and she will get right to business. You can be more specific if you'd like and say "Alexa, play Game of Thrones". She has you covered.

Another benefit of the Cube's connection with Alexa is the ability to control your cable box. If you tell Alexa to "tune into CBS", your cable box comes on and soon, your channel follows. Alexa is limited in generic programming with certain apps like Hulu though. For example, you can't say "Alexa, go to the Braves game" but eventually, as more and more companies are working to evolve their products in conjunction with Alexa, more skills will be available.

Without ever leaving your couch, you can use the Cube to make purchases and find information like - how far is it from the Earth to the moon or ask it to play music. There is a remote if you should get tired of the voice activation commands or to scroll through all the pages of movie options. The remote does come in handy but why keep up with yet another controller when you can just speak out loud what you want?

While the Cube is an already amazing device, Amazon already has plans to take the Fire TV Stick to 4K and beyond. With an upgrade in sound, picture, and content, Amazon wants to take the digital entertainment experience to a brand new, immersive level. With enhanced Alexa voice recognition and an even wider range of compatible IR-enabled devices, you'll have even more control over your home than ever before with the all-new Alexa Voice Remote. This new remote will allow Alexa the ability to switch TV inputs, change compatible cable box functions, sound bars, and much, much more.

Regardless of what your preferred device is, what type of programming you are looking for, or if you're at home or on the go, Amazon has your entertainment needs taken care of.

With so many options to choose from and with the help of Alexa, you'll wonder why you didn't get your Amazon devices communicating sooner.

Chapter 5: Free Time for Kids and Parents

Amazon knows you want reliability, efficiency, and affordability, but what about peace of mind? Technology is a great way for you to receive on demand entertainment but what about for your kids? Making sure they have a learning environment that is kid-friendly is what Amazon had in mind when they created the FreeTime Unlimited program.

Through a variety of devices like your child's phone or tablet, you can rest assured that they are reading, watching, and learning through content that you choose and that is appropriate for their age.

Amazon's FreeTime program gives parents reassurance in knowing that when their child is on the internet, they are viewing content that is age appropriate. FreeTime gives a customizable experience for your child based on your specifications.

You can choose from three different age groups ranging from 3 – 12, and from reliable and trustworthy sources like Disney, Nickelodeon, and Sesame Street. The program also allows the child to have their own profile set up so that when they log on, they will receive information based on their preferred viewing.

Parents are able to set daily time limits, modify internet search behavior, pause the device, as well as monitor profile activity. FreeTime goes even further in giving parents control by allowing multiple child profiles to be tailored to each individual child. Age filters allow the parent the ability to ensure different age groups are only seeing age appropriate information for their age group.

Ages 3 to 5   Ages 6 to 8   Ages 9 to 12

There is even the option for parents to limit games and videos being played until after certain educational goals are met. There is also the capability of allowing only reading while eliminating access to games. Within the program, there is no access to social media and purchases can't be made without parent approval.

After choosing which plan you want to set up for your child, you will then be prompted to create a child profile for them. Here you enter basic things like their name, their date of birth, their gender, and then an icon that you (or your little one) can decide represents them the best.

From there you can see do all the parent things that go on behind the scenes, like manage your payment methods and subscription settings. You can also get detailed information about the program; get help if you are having difficulty setting up program, and contact customer service directly.

Manage FreeTime Unlimited Subscription

Modify 1-Click Settings

Cancel Subscription

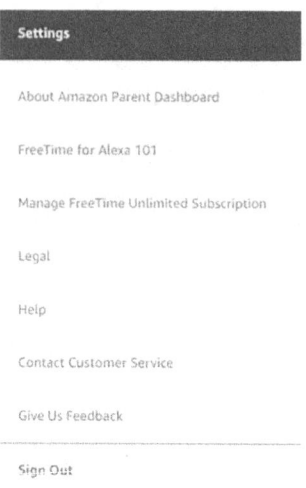

To go to your child's main profile screen, click on the white arrow within the Parent Dashboard banner.

Going to the next screen allows you to set the guidelines you want specifically for your child. You can also see any communication your child has had and the specific time that has been spent within each section.

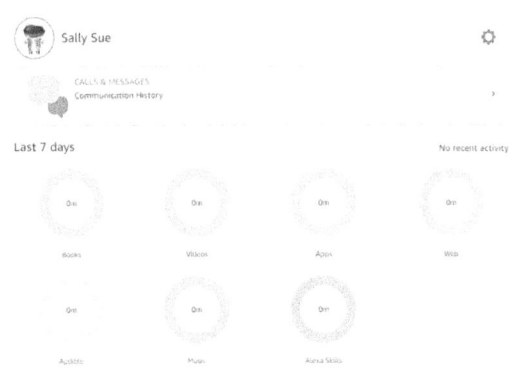

By clicking on each individual section, you can see specific information for each. For example, if you click on the Videos section, what you will see is any activity that your child has had.

In this instance, the child has had no activity within this section in the past 90 days. This can be specifically helpful if you are trying to help your child learn a specific skill. You can see just how much time they are spending within each task and can gauge their progress or where they may need extra help.

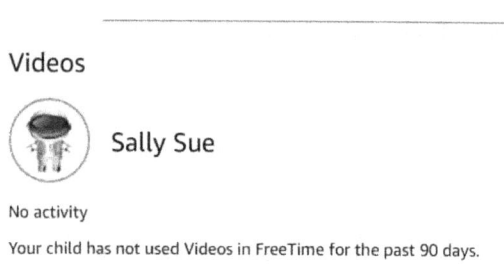

To see even more information about your child's activity, you can select the settings section on the bottom of the profile.

From here you have the ability to grant access or change limitations to a variety of different things. This can be especially helpful as your child ages, should your content choices change, or if you just want a full range of control over what your child is able to see and do. The settings screen allows you to have complete access to anything and everything your child sees and does. Not only is this reassuring for you as a parent but it protects the safety and security of your child which is ultimately the most important feature.

Amazon has gone to great lengths to make sure that parents have as much control over the safety of their children as possible. However, sometimes technical issues do come up with app updates and things involving the specific devices.

Things that you can adjust include:

- ***Adding Content*** – Share digital content purchases you have made through Amazon with the FreeTime program within 30 minutes.

- ***Set Daily Time Limits*** – You have the freedom to adjust daily limits by the hour, for the weekdays or weekends, total screen time limits, educational goals, and if certain goals aren't met, you can limit what they have available in their profile.

- ***Modify Web Browser*** – You can set what types of websites they are able to view, you can pre-approve content, and enable or disable cookies.

- ***In-App Purchasing*** – Requires password and is only available on certain devices.

- ***Alexa Settings*** – You can even adjust the things that Alexa will listen to regarding your Smart Home and surround Echo devices.
- ***And more***…

At the bottom of your child's profile right above the additional settings section, you will see blue text that is actually a link to take you to a detailed troubleshooting screen. This screen shows you what you should be seeing when you are in the parent dashboard, what version you should be using for both you and your child within the FreeTime program, the steps to update the app for both IOS and Android devices, and to let you know that any Fire TV devices should update automatically.

Tap on a category (above) to view your child's past activity. Not seeing your child's activity?

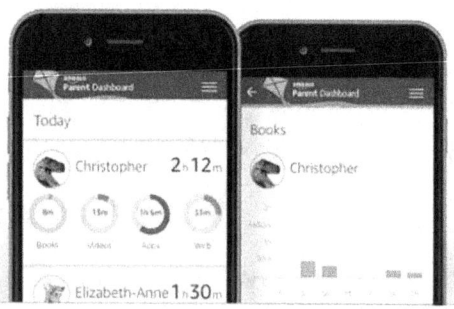

On this screen, if you click on the text you will automatically be directed to the app store to install the latest version. This way you will be able to see your child's activity in no time.

What about the Teens?

All this information has been geared towards the younger members of your family, but what about the teens in your house? How is Amazon letting you use your account so that the young adults in your house feel like an individual while still being part of the family? Now for teens age 13 – 17, Amazon has developed a way for the younger members of your family have responsibility while still being under the protected account of mom and dad.

While having the freedom to make purchases under your Prime account can be a great benefit, it can also be a costly luxury that sends the family spending budget through the roof. Amazon has developed a way so that your teen can have their own wish list, make their own purchases, but gives you the freedom to approve or deny any purchase made with a simple text message or email.

Giving your teen access to your Prime benefits is as simple as sending an invitation. By sending an invitation link to your teen's email from your main Amazon Prime account, they will be able to use specific benefits of your account without impacting your purchases or account details. They have to provide their account information like date of birth and phone number but after that, they are able to receive common Prime benefits that you are accustomed to. Things like free two-day shipping, Prime Video, and Twitch Video are now available to your teen at no additional cost.

Setting up your account so that your teen has access is as simple as going to https://www.amazon.com/cr/forteens

From this site, parents will have the ability to send their teens a message to create their own account or teens will be able to send their parents a notification to let them join the family account. The teen login is separate from the parent's login so neither are bumping into each other with purchases or device activity, but the parent always has the final say in regard to purchases.

Below is a simple breakdown of how this new way of teen purchasing works.

- Using their own logins, teens are able to make purchases.
- Parents are notified through either text message or email with all details regarding purchase info.

- Parents can approve or deny any and all purchase as well as set automatic spending limits with a simple reply of 'Y' or 'N'.
- Both the parent and the teen receive delivery date info.

Amazon knows your family is the most important thing to you. They also want you to be in complete control of spending, viewing, and internet safety at all times. That's why they've made it so that no matter the age of your child, you are well aware of what they are doing so that you can help them make safe and secure choices.

By setting limits, protection guidelines, and having constant up-to-date notifications, you can be sure that your account information and your child's spending activity are protected and balanced.

Chapter 6: Alexa, Your Personal Assistant

Wouldn't it be nice to have someone that we could give directions to have them take care of the mundane tasks so that we can focus on more important matters at hand? What if her name was Alexa? The Amazon Echo voice-recognition system or "Alexa" has been designed with over 10,000 skills right out of the box with more to follow. Her main goal is helping you manage your day-to-day living tasks with ease but the things she's able to do will amaze you. Read on to find out more.

From programming the lights to accessing your music library, Alexa (named after the archaic library of Alexandria) has been designed with the capabilities to make your household run smooth and with as little effort as possible on your part.

By now, you already know some of the things Alexa is capable of doing but how much more benefit can you get out of the digital-assistant? Alexa not only gives you information on the weather, but she can also connect to your music library, to your Smart TV, you can listen to your Kindle choices as audiobooks through Alexa as well. Amazon is even getting to the point where you can connect home appliances to Alexa and she will operate them based on your voice activated commands. Alexa is truly the assistant of the future but how can we utilize her skills so that she is as useful as intended?

Alexa allows you the ability to connect to your favorite programs with just a matter of a few specific commands. Things like ordering pizza, turning off the lights, or cooking popcorn are being revamped every day. Who wouldn't want to connect to their Amazon account and make the mundane tasks of daily living that much more exciting?

While Alexa has the capability of doing the basics for you, she can also help you communicate and control the many different devices that you have in your house. Things like your smart lights, the smart lock, the smart doorbell, and so many more appliances and devices are being created so that they are able to function with Alexa. As we discussed in prior chapters, things like operating the TV or playing digital music are great skills but by utilizing Alexa for more than just entertainment functions, you can start to see a whole new world where Alexa will start making everyday life much easier. At least she can take some of the last minute or inconveniencing tasks out of the equation.

Before you can start giving Alexa voice commands, you need to connect her to your Wi-Fi. Just open up your favorite web browser, follow the steps we've listed for you below, and soon you won't know how you went without having a personal assistant for so long.

| Connecting Alexa to your Wi-Fi | 1. Go to https://alexa.amazon.com 2. Log in 3. Plug in and turn on Echo 4. Wait for orange ring |

	light
	5. Hold down action button on Echo for 5 seconds
	6. In the browser app, click settings
	7. Choose set up new device
	8. Choose your Echo type
	9. Choose your Wi-Fi network
	10. Click connect

You will find that there are multiple device brands that all work well with Alexa with varying prices and perks. You can best determine what will work for you and your budget but for now, we will only cover the many ways Alexa helps take care of simple things and how you can start reaping the benefits of Alexa through your Amazon account. By now you've set up your music, your reading, and your kids are all set for their learning adventure. Now, we're going to add everything together through the Amazon experience that is Alexa.

To use Alexa to her fullest capabilities as they stand right now, here are a few things to get you started. The way she operates is you give her a command, and she gets to work gathering information or by communicating with devices you have in your house. For example, she can play radio stations, set timers and alarms, relay news reports, make calls to cellphones, and like Siri on the iPhone, she has a sense of humor.

In previous chapters, we touched briefly on the ways Alexa is capable of controlling different technical outlets in your home. Here we will expand on just how she is able to connect and interact with the current available options.

Alexa Plays the Beats

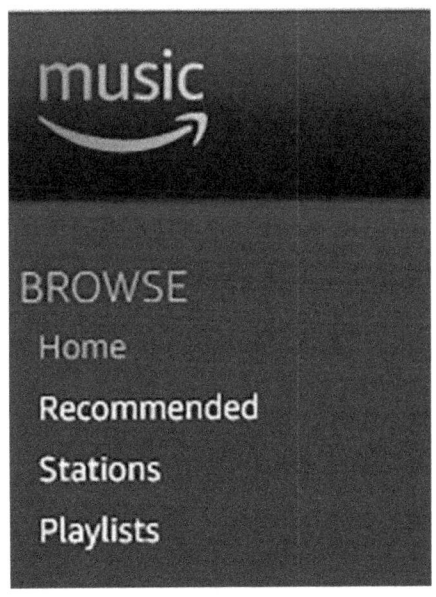

One of the most common ways that Alexa is used is for her ability to play music. By giving her certain commands she can play songs, channels, bands, and even specific eras all by voice command controls. Simply by activating Alexa, you will have the freedom to control your music library anywhere in your house.

What if you have a different account for your music through Spotify or Pandora? No worries, you can connect those accounts to Alexa as well for your listening pleasure. Just go back to the browser app that you used to connect Alexa to your Wi-Fi (https://alexa.amazon.com), choose Settings>Accounts>Music & Media.

Note: this can be done from your computer browser or through the app on your tablet/phone.)

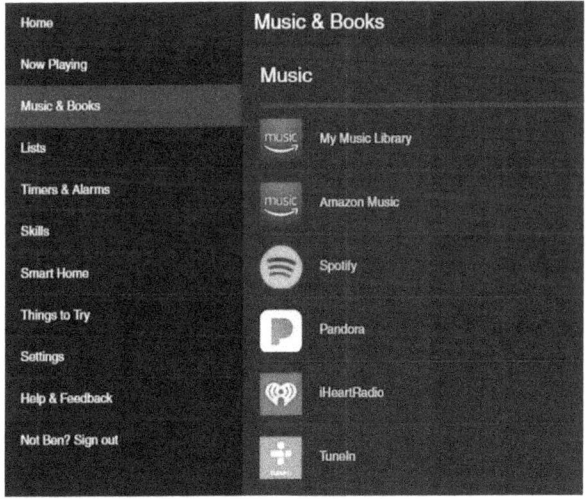

If you don't have a subscription through another service, or you don't pay for the Amazon music subscription services, you can still listen to your previously purchased or downloaded music through the Bluetooth feature.

What's wrong, Alexa?

If you find that you have followed all the above steps and Alexa won't play your music, you should try restarting your Echo. Just unplug it for a few minutes and then plug it back in. If that doesn't work, try removing the services you connected and reconnecting them. If you've tried all the troubleshooting and you still can't get Alexa to function properly, you can contact Amazon support specifically for Alexa. They will have you and Alexa up and running in no time.

Alexa Is the New Desktop Assistant

Using Alexa to help you stay organized for both personal and business activities has never been easier. Now that you have her connected to your Wi-Fi, Alexa can keep up with appointments; make shopping lists, find information, read the latest news report, save recipes, set timers, and more on your PC.

Alexa is more than capable of helping you keep up with your responsibilities. Once she's connected just speak freely the tasks you need her to complete and watch her work her magic. As Alexa's technology evolves and new features are being added, you will be amazed at how effective her skills are in assisting you.

Give Alexa an Apple

Not only is Alexa a great accessory for your PC but she is also capable of functioning with the browser on your Mac computer as well. The steps to connecting her are similar to that of the PC counterpart. You just need to access the link (https://alexa.amazon.com), make sure Alexa is connected to your Wi-Fi, and then let Alexa get to work.

If you happen to have one of Amazon's Fire tablets, the Alexa app should be already installed for even easier access. Otherwise, you can download it free from the app store on your specific device.

What's on TV, Alexa?

Being able to control your TV with Alexa could potentially feel like you have stepped into a live action episode of the Jetsons. You'll be able to go through menus with ease and be able to access your favorite programs a lot faster. Even though her technology is essentially hassle free, there are a still a few places where she needs a little help. Nonetheless, having an assistant to eliminate all the frustrations involved with programming will definitely make movie night a lot easier.

Newer Fire TV devices automatically include a remote for Alexa. This allows you to speak directly into the microphone to issue your voice commands. If you have multiple Fire TV devices that you want connected, you will have to decide which device you want Alexa to use to control the TV.

Follow the steps below to set up extra Fire TV devices:

Setting up Multiple Fire TV devices	1. Go to https://alexa.amazon.com or open Alexa app on your phone
2. Select Menu Button- top left
3. Select Music, Video, and Books
4. Choose Fire TV from Video section
5. Select 'Manage Devices'
6. Select 'Link Another Fire TV'
7. Choose the Fire TV you want
8. Choose set up new device (only one Fire TV can be controlled per Alexa)
9. If you have multiple

	Alexa devices, choose the one you want to control the TV.

Now that you've got Alexa set up on the TV, you can start asking Alexa to connect you to your desired programs. Alexa even has technology to work with some of the common favorite apps like Netflix and Hulu. She isn't advanced yet to the point where she communicates with every app, but as her skills grow, so will her communication capacity. Alexa also doesn't have the capability to scroll through search results via voice command in some apps, but if you see something and you want more info, just ask Alexa to play it. The more specific you are in your request; the better Alexa's results will be.

Example commands for Alexa include (there are a lot more!):

- "Alexa, search for dramas on Netflix"
- "Alexa, search for mysteries on Hulu"
- "Alexa, show me Harry Potter movies"

If you want to take your TV operation through Alexa to an even greater level, the Fire TV Cube can help. The Fire TV Cube is created specifically for controlling your TV in combination with Alexa. Unlike other Fire TV devices, the Cube allows Alexa to scroll through information through the voice command "Alexa, show more." Alexa is also capable of operating your traditional TV services from a variety of providers through the Cube. Providers like Comcast, AT-T, and DirecTV are just a few of the providers that allow you to watch local and live channels. To set this feature up go to Settings>Equipment Control>Manage Equipment>Add Equipment, and then choose either Cable or Satellite.

Now you can let Alexa do all the work!

Conclusion

Thank you for making it through to the end of *How to Add a Device to My Kindle Account,* let's hope it was informative and able to provide you with all of the tools you need to achieve your goals, whatever they may be. The book is over, but your fun has just begun with your new digitally connected world. From your TV, to the computer, to your own virtual assistant, you are well on your way to having a digitally connected home.

The next step is to get your Amazon account connected to your devices. The sooner you can get everything hooked up, downloaded, and logged in, the sooner you are able to have a voice activated, hands free house that your whole family will want to be a part of. Whether you decide on one device or an entire collection of devices, this book will hopefully help you understand and connect your house in a digitally smart way.

Once you've made the toughest decision of all, deciding which device you are going to use first, be sure and check back to the tools and tips in this book. The breakdown of each step that's required to get the devices connected, as well as the detailed descriptions and what can be expected moving forward will definitely help you in making the best decision for your household's needs.

Finally, if you found this book useful in any way, a review on Amazon is always appreciated!

Mark Howard

Check Out Other Books

Go here to check out other related books that might interest you:

Kindle Fire HD 10 Manual: The Complete User Guide with Instructions, Tutorial to Unlock the True Potential of Your Kindle HD10 Fire Tablet in 30 Minutes
https://amzn.to/2zVr3rq

Alexa: How to Use Your Amazon Alexa Devices New, Essential User Guide for Amazon Echo and Alexa (The Complete User Guide-Alexa & Echo Show Setup and Tips)
https://amzn.to/2NuBeFe

Kindle Fire HD 8 & 10 Tablet with Alexa: How to Use Kindle Fire HD, the Complete User Guide with Step-by-Step Instructions

https://amzn.to/2NMvarM

Amazon Echo Show User Guide: Amazon Echo Show with Step-by-Step Instructions, Amazon Echo Setup (The Complete User Guide)
https://amzn.to/2NOSdm7

Kindle Fire HD Manual: The Complete Tutorial and User Guide for Your New Kindle Fire HD Device in 30 Minutes
https://amzn.to/2AAuwMw

Fire Stick: Essential User Guide for Amazon Fire Stick, How to Unlock Your Fire Stick Like a Pro (Amazon Fire TV, Amazon Fire TV Stick, Amazon Fire TV Cube)

https://amzn.to/2Mypamo

Amazon Echo Dot - 2nd Generation Amazon Echo Dot with Alexa: How to Unlock the True Potential of Your Echo Dot, Learn to Use Your Echo Dot Like a Pro

https://amzn.to/2KZ6VVL

Kindle Fire HD8 Tablet: How to Use Kindle Fire HD, the Complete User Guide with Step-by-Step Instructions, Tutorial to Unlock the True Potential of Your Device in 30 Minutes
https://amzn.to/2Lctd6E

Alexa and Amazon Echo Dot: The Complete User Guide with Step by Step Instructions, User Guide to Master Your Amazon Echo Dot and Alexa (Two Book Bundle)
https://amzn.to/2BPTpUU

Kindle Fire HD 8 & 10 Instructions: The Complete User Guide with Step by Step Instructions, Learn to Master Your Kindle Fire HD 8 & 10 Tablet in 1 Hour (Two Book Bundle)
https://amzn.to/2oi4QeK

How to Delete Books off Your Kindle: Essential Guide on How to Delete Books from Your Kindle Device and Other Useful Tips
https://amzn.to/2MJl27s

Machine Learning: An Introduction for Beginners, User Guide to Build Intelligent Systems
https://amzn.to/2CfGL1U

Deep Learning: Concepts and Applications for Beginners Guide to Building Intelligent Systems
https://amzn.to/2NPK0S0

Machine Learning and Deep Learning: Essential User Guide to Learn and

Understand Machine Learning and Deep Learning Effectively (Two Book Bundle)
https://amzn.to/2QzroV3

www.ingramcontent.com/pod-product-compliance
Lightning Source LLC
Chambersburg PA
CBHW071555220526
45469CB00003B/1024